Words of Faith

A Way to
Connect You to
God

About the Book

The poems of this book relate topics relevant to Christians, such as faith, hope, perseverance, overcoming, worship, love, peace, biblical stories, etc.

Many of the poems were based on preaching by the pastors: Joel Osteen and Danilo Montero (Lakewood Church, Houston, Texas), Dante Gebel (River Church, Los Angeles, California) and Andrea Vargas (Avalanche Missões, Vitória, Espírito Santo, Brazil); and on YouTube's channels: Guided Morning Prayers (@guidedmorningprayers), Above Inspiration (@aboveinspiration) and Joyce Meyer Ministries (@joyccmeyer).

Table of Contents

Interminable Fights

The walk is hard, and the journey is painful,
There is no rest, and there are always new battles.
Some of them seem interminable,
Some of them seem invincible.

I am fighting day after day, and nothing changes,
I always do my best, and the fight continues.
This fight drains all my strength and wears out me,
I do not see the light anymore; I do not see good things.

New difficulties come, and the fight has no end,
The despair comes, and in this way, I cannot stand.
I cry; I get desperate, and I claim help,
I need someone to help me in this battle.

A small light at the end of the tunnel is seen,
Someone will help me; the hope is renewed.
The person gets close and extends their hand,
The words said talk directly to my heart.

The Lord came to my fight and will help me,
He will give me strength and help me to win.
God says to me that bad days will always exist,
He comforts me saying He always will be here.

I breathe relieved because I know I am not lonely,
In all battles, the Lord will be with me.
I will face all the fights with my head up high,
The victory is guaranteed with the Lord on my side.

The Great Threat

We must be careful at all moments,
We are surrounded by many threats.
Many things are trying to hit us,
Many situations can hurt us.

Among all the dangers, the cobras are the worst ones,
With their words, they launch terrible venom.
There is a source of curse in their mouths,
A destruction work is working in their tongues.

The cobra contaminates everything around,
It destroys its victim by taking it to the dust and ground.
The cobra spreads discord, sadness and lies,
Their only objective is to destroy victims' lives.

That one who is attacked live in great affliction,
They need help; they need protection.
There is only an antidote to save the victim,
There is only a Savior to that life.

This one is the Lord God Almighty,
He will destroy the cobra, frustrating all their deeds.
Everything that they have done will be destroyed,
It will be as if they had never existed.

The Lord God will take care of the one who was attacked,
On His powerful arms, the Lord will carry them.
God will turn his affliction into happiness,
The Lord will take them from despair to peacefulness.

The protection of God will be over that life,
God will protect them from everything against their lives.
No matter how many cobras try to attack them,
The Lord will eliminate each of them.

The Best Help

Each person lives things that nobody can imagine,
Each one has their great battles for fighting.
And in most of the time, these battles are heavy,
The person needs help not to be defeated.

Sometimes it lacks support for their emotional,
The person needs help to overcome the chaos.
They can be tired, discouraged and hopeless,
They think they will not win, and this will be endless.

If we see someone like that, we can do only one thing,
There is only one way to help that life.
We must ask for help from the one who can do everything,
We must ask for help from the Owner of all things.

The Lord is attentive to our petition,
If we ask, He will help in that situation.
God will start a transformation in that life,
The hope will be born as a new sunrise.

God will give vitality to that one who was tired,
The Lord will give courage to the one who was exhausted.
The person will be amazed by their transformation,
And all this started with our petition.

Never doubt about what you can do to help,
You can do your best: pray.
The One who hears our petition is faithful and wonderful,
The God Almighty is always hearing you.

The Prayer

Prayer is a fundamental part of the Christian life,
For many reasons, each one keeps praying.
They always pray asking for some blessing,
And there are also prayers asking for pardon.
God will hear all prayers, no matter the reason.

The great majority of the prayers are personal requests,
We want to receive from God His blessing and peace.
Sometimes, we pray for our beloved ones,
For their needs, we pray and make petitions.

Besides these, there are others who deserve our prayers,
Everyone we know deserves our care.
We should pray for the people we see every day,
We should ask God to bless their lives and ways.

Even not knowing what each one is living,
God knows all things and will give His blessing.
We do not even need to talk about our petition,
We only need to pray and trust in God and His action.

As Christians, we know that our prayers have power,
We know that at the right time, God will give His answer.
May we have the disposition to keep on praying,
Because God will always be listening.

There is no Tomorrow

Tomorrow is a day that will never exist,
Because when we arrive there, today will be.
It is a big illusion to let something for tomorrow,
We do not know if we will have another day to go.

Our only certainty is what we live in this very today,
Today is the only moment to fix our lives and ways.
Do not live thinking you will never die,
Think that on this very day, it can arrive.

What comes next if this takes place?
Where will your spirit go after you have passed away?
Are you sure what awaits you on the other side?
Will be something glorious? Or a tormented life?

Eliminate this doubt from your heart today,
Bend your knees, raise your hands and pray.
Cry out to God wholeheartedly,
Pray to the Lord and ask His forgiveness.

God is merciful and will hear you,
The forgiveness for your sins, He will give you.
The Lord God will give you His salvation,
God will free you from doubt and condemnation.

Stop what you are doing and pray to the Lord now,

Maybe God is calling you right now.

Heed the voice of the Lord and obey Him,

God wants to care for you for the entire eternity.

Keep Going Ahead

Before God, everything has a perfect time,
He knows when all things will be right.
Even when we cannot notice with our sight,
God is working and is always blessing our lives.

If we trust in God, there is no reason for desperation,
We can see complete chaos in our situation,
However, this cannot disturb our faith in God,
Because everything is under the control of the Lord.

Maybe this terrible situation will teach us something,
Maybe this suffering time is necessary for learning.
God would never allow anything to harm us,
He allows things to happen because He trusts us.

Besides trusting us, God also strength us for the fight,
He gives us the means to win and protection for our lives.
God is going ahead of this battle to open the way,
He is preparing our victory, and this will be amazing.

We will see that it was worth it to live all these things,
We will learn that all we have lived has a meaning.
The things we have learned will continue to help us,
This learning will help when a new battle comes to us.

Contaminated Church

Brazilian Christian church lives in a sad situation,
It has allowed entering into it the contamination.
Letting what is right and going to corruption,
The worst thing: they state that God is in action.

The church involved itself with dirty and immoral ones,
People thirsty for violence who take off peace of everyone.
The church established a new god and gave him adoration,
The church believes that a politician is its salvation.

Before this man, the church bowed,
There is a new "savior", and Jesus is ignored.
The "savior" is someone who will change the nation,
A man who will lead people to their liberation.

The church got blind after hearing a cheering speech,
As a supreme lord, everyone started to defend him.
In his defense, all can lie, attack and deceive,
They even can kill if it is necessary.

There is no limit to please the new god of "Christians",
He deserves all sacrifices, fasting, prayer and petitions.
His followers say that he was sent from the Lord,
Because of it, he deserves all respect, praise, and love.

Many "Christians" continue believing in this lie,
To a corrupt one, they are dedicating their lives.
They are very far from the will of the Lord,
All worship and praise belong only to God.

Change of Thought

Some situations seem to be our end,
We feel we cannot do anything there.
There is nothing good at the place,
We think: it is over; soon, my death will take place.

However, God did not leave us there to die,
The Lord put us there to see changes in our lives.
God wants to see our growth in that place,
He knows that even in difficulty we can advance.

When we start to see the situation from a different sight,
The Lord begins to open our hearts and minds.
We will be calm and confident in the Lord,
Certain that we are always helped by God.

We will see that all the complaints of the past were useless,
We complained because we were fearful and hopeless.
At that time, we still did not understand,
We did not believe that God put us on that path.

After we understand what we should do,
We will work to make something new.
We will be able to do things that we had not thought of,
We will achieve what we had never dreamed of.

But God

I am very weak,
But God is with me.
I can do anything,
But God can do all things.

Everything seems impossible,
But God does everything possible.
There is no exit in my way,
But God creates a new way.

I cannot overcome my situation,
But God can win on any occasion.
My anguish is discouraging me,
But God is strengthening me.

Everything seems to be against my life,
But God is walking by my side.
I do not know what I have to do,
But God tells me the best to do.

I have many uncertainties,
But God has all certainties.
I do not know what will take place,
But God will always be with me.

Transformations

Jesus is a powerful name,
If you meet and learn from Him,
Your life will never be the same,
You will gain many new things.

He will be your master and guide,
You will access a sea of knowledge.
You will be able to live a fresh life,
The infinite wisdom, you will get.

His teachings will be engraved on you,
The radiance of your mind will glow.
No foolishness bullet will touch you.
It does not matter how many they throw.

Go ahead with Jesus in your way,
With Him, you will never feel alone.
Never forget the miracles He performed.
You will be accompanied by the Might One.

Situation and Behavior

We live hard, tough, and complicated situations,
Situations in which justice is not in action.
Evil is free and acts in all and everyone with ease,
There is no slightest trace of righteousness, truth, or peace.

All seems to be rotten and corrupted,
All good feelings have been destroyed.
Vengeance gathers like the water in a dam,
All cruelty options are on hand.

Each of us can choose what we want to do,
Each one can choose our way to get through.
All is allowed; it seems not to have any condemnation,
The darkest desires are available for our utilization.

Even though we are faced with so many possibilities,
We must flee from all these iniquities.
We cannot behave like this generation,
We are the chosen people by God for salvation.

We are the chosen children and heirs of light,
We are the elected nation that will dwell with Christ.
Even if no one does what is right and fair,
We must be and make a difference in this world out there.

Our mission is to show that there is still goodness,

Showing the world that there is still happiness.

Let everyone know of the love and justice of the Lord,

Let everyone know there is a Savior.

Comprehending the Moment

There are moments in which we are imprisoned,
We feel we are arrested and defenseless.
From all sides, we are oppressed and crushed.

All things seem to come against our life,
The days are chaotic, hard, and very cruel.
There is no exit even though we do our best in the fight.

We bow our heads and start to cry,
The harsh and brutal fight could overwhelm us.
We look ahead; there is no exit in our sight.

We think that it is time to give up everything,
We consider that we already were defeated.
There is no use facing the world or keep fighting.

We cry out to God and show our hearts' suffering,
We say to Him everything that is taking place.
We pour out infinite tears; in great distress, we are living.

The Lord is so loving and understands our plight,
Gently He explains to us our path.
Nothing was in vain; all was a big training for life.

The Lord prepared us for the great day,

He trained us to receive a big blessing.

He empowered us in His infinite wisdom's ways.

We understand that everything was planned,

There was purpose in everything we have lived.

Our tough times were for something to be learned.

The Detachment and the Return

All was very different at the beginning of my journey,
I wanted to do all the work spontaneously.
There was no need for anyone to ask me,
There was no need for anyone to call me.
I was always on hand to do all kinds of work,
I dedicated myself passionately with all my effort.

The time passed, and my interest decreased,
I did not see my job as something useful and required.
I thought that there were other people to do it,
I thought I was only one more; nobody would need me.
I moved away from all work and obligations,
I sought other opportunities, other options.

Each moment, I was farther from the Lord,
With each passing day, I was more distant from His love.
My lips no longer sang His praise,
My life no long reflected His glory, splendor, and grace.
There was no difference between holy and profane,
There was no distinction between spiritual and mundane.

I went through a path that would lead me to true happiness,
A road to a new life with prosperity and fullness.
This route would lead me to a marvelous kingdom,
On which I would reign mighty and strong.
I reached the highest level of conquer and realization,
I sat on a throne to contemplate my perfection.

That world had all I had ever dreamed of,
Yet, its pleasures and gifts, I did not enjoy.
Everything seemed to lead me to a joy never seen before,
But the things offered did not satisfy me anymore.
After I had experienced infinite wonders,
I felt in my life an equally infinite emptiness.

It lacked in me the essential, that gave sense to my life,
I was missing the perfect love of Christ.
After many misadventures, I recognized my sin,
I was alone, poor, and naked; I needed God with me.
I humbled myself before Him and begged His forgiveness,
As a loving father, He extended His hand showing kindness.

I returned to the path of the Lord, and today I am renewed,
God cleansed me from all wickedness and all sin.
I do all for the Lord with extreme zeal and dedication,
All the days, I acknowledge and thank His salvation.
There are no words to describe my acknowledgment,
I can only show it with adoration and praise in all moments.

The Joy of Confidence

Today will be an awesome day,
Because God is ahead in my way.

He will protect me,
He will guide me,
He will lead me,
He will stay with me.

The Lord is faithful in all His promises,
He promised that He will always be with me.
God promised steadfast protection,
He made a covenant for everlasting generations.

God will provide everything,
God will rid me of all bad things.
I have no concern; I trust in Him.

Even if something rises against my life,
I have the mighty God in this fight.
The Lord will never fail with me,
Because the Lord loves me.

There is no reason for fear,
There is no reason to pour out tears.
All things are subjected to the Lord,
All things obey the Almighty God.

I will always believe in the God of my salvation,

I will always be part of His Holy Nation.

I wait anxiously for the day I will dwell with Him,

That amazing day when my spirit will embrace Him.

After

I have always heard about you,

But I never followed either your path or you.

I never wanted to stay by your side,

I always thought I would be tied.

I wanted to continue enjoying my freedom,

I did not want to live as a believer; with restrictions.

I already knew about their way of living,

There are rules and limitations in everything.

I did not want to live in this kind of prison,

My mind wanted to live without any preoccupation.

I denied all invitations I have received,

In Christian service, I have never appeared.

I invented excuses for those who invited me,

I said that in the next service, I would be.

I created the most incredible excuses,

Most of them were very confused.

I knew that people did not believe what I said,

However, they were sure I will not go to the place.

The invitations continued, and I had to innovate,

I invented new things to escape.

I said that was not the hour for my conversion to God,

One day, in the future, I will deliver my heart to the Lord.

Those who heard it always have advised me:
"Take care; you don't know how long you'll be here."
I replied that I was not concerned about it,
If God loves me, He will give me an opportunity.

I suppose that people were tired of me,
No other invitation came to me.
Finally, no one came to disturb me,
I could do everything; I was at peace.
Without knowing God, my life was going on,
I left it for last; I planned to become one of His sons.

Without warning, life hit me terribly,
My existence has been erased quickly.
In a moment, I was walking,
In the next one, I was on the ground bleeding.

My strength and vitality were escaping rapidly,
I had no chance to regret it.
Everything had finished; I died in my sin,
In a terrible hell, I will be thrown in.
I could prevent all of this.

The Tree That Could Not Grow

Like a tree, I want to grow,
A showy and excellent plant, I want to show.
Let my branches spread out to all sides,
And my treetop and trunk reach the skies.

Growing is my innermost heart's desire,
This thought catches my imagination all the time.
I always seek the best soil for my development,
I always seek ways for self–improvement.

I seek pure water streams constantly,
They will supply my needs permanently.
I do my best to achieve success,
But I am not growing; nothing has any effect.

After carefully analyzing my situation,
I discovered I live in a sad condition.
I discovered I do not grow because I am surrounded,
I do not grow because I am being obfuscated.

There are many big and old trees in the way,
They always try to thwart my plans every day.
None of them supports the way I try to go,
But all of them criticize me when I try to grow.

They say growth is not meant for me,

They say all my actions will do for nothing.

Long ago, these trees stopped dreaming,

Now, their mission is trying to discourage me.

I cannot hear them, I cannot stop to fight,

I need exceptional help to improve my life.

This wonderful help will come from that one who created me,

The help of the gardener, the Lord, I will receive.

God will open the way to my growth,

Taking off all that was covering me; all the shadows.

The Lord always believes in what I can do,

He always blesses my way and makes something good.

Like the gardener, God cared about His creation,

He poured out His blessing and removed any limitations.

I have learned I must trust and believe only in the Lord,

He is the only one who gifts me true love.

God is the unique who will always help me,

My growth will never stop since I continue with Him.

Thank You

Thank you, Lord, for one more chance.
Thank you for living one more day under your loving glance.

Thank you for always protecting me,
Thank you for always helping me.

Thank you for everything I possess,
Thank you for all the food that I have.

Thank you for the ceiling over me,
Thank you for the clothes that warm me.

Thank you for your infinite faithfulness and kindness,
Thank you for keeping my life under your blessings.

Thank you for choosing me for salvation,
Thank you for giving me your unction.

Thank you for the privilege of praising You,
Thank you for the privilege of adoring You.

Thank you for always guiding me,
Thank you for always being with me.

Thank you for all happiness lived,
Thank you for all promises fulfilled.

Thank you for my gifts received,
Thank you for the immeasurable love of Christ.

Thank you for being my God, Father, and Lord,
Thank you for your infinite and incomparable love.

Thank you is what I will always say,
Thank you will be my most repeated phrase.

He

There is someone who can do everything,
He can change any history,
There are no limits to His actions,
There are no barriers that can stop him.

For Him, there is no very long distance,
Or abyss terribly deep,
There is no mountain He cannot climb,
Nothing can put Him away from His objective.

He desires to be known and loved,
He desires that people know Him by name,
He desires to be the best friend,
That one who people tell secrets to.

He is always willing to hear,
He never gets tired of anyone,
His strength and ability are infinite,
And His goodness is bigger than all.

Oh! How He longs for your approach!
He waits for you patiently.
He is calling you right now,
He desires that you be with Him.

Jesus extends His kind hand to you,
He is smiling while watching you.
Accept the invitation and live by His side,
Your life will undergo a great change.

Where there was sadness there will be joy,
Where there was weep it will be born hope,
Where there was discouragement will emerge strength,
Where there was a fear will overflow courage.

And whenever something comes against you,
There will be no reason to be concerned.
The Lord Jesus will be in your way,
All battles will be won.

Meet this marvelous Lord,
Allow a turnaround in your world.
Leave behind what does not work,
And follow through a new and beautiful road.

For the change happening,
You need to make a decision.
You need to cry to the Lord,
You must invite Him to your life.

Cry out wholeheartedly and live something new,
Let Jesus enter and begin the change.
He will do whatever it takes,
And in the end, only He will be necessary.

An Extraordinary Day

That seemed to be only one more day,
One like all the others in his life's way.
That man was brought to his place,
He lived there begging for someone's grace.

The poor man had been born lame and disabled,
He could not walk; he was always carried.
He depended on everyone for all the things,
He was free, but there was a sad prison for him.

At a special place, the man was placed,
He was left at the temple, in the Beautiful gate.
He expected that day to be usual,
Staying on the ground already seemed natural.

He saw all the people and asked for alms from them,
He wanted only a crumb to satiate him at that moment.
In his life, there was no hope or perspective,
To be alive at the end of that day was his wish.

Two men passed through that gate,
He extended his hand, and some alms; he waited.
His life began to change at that moment,
The attention of them was on that man.

The men asked him to raise his sight,
They could see the face of suffering life.
The man waited to receive something,
He did not imagine what was happening.

He did not know who those men represented,
He had no idea about the power inside of them.
Peter and John were directed to be right there,
At that hour, the glory of Jesus would act.

Peter did not have silver or gold to donate,
But he had Jesus Christ; a miracle would take place.
In the name of Jesus Christ, Peter declared to him:
"Walk, you are receiving the Lord's healing."

The healing happened instantaneously,
The change occurred immediately.
His feet returned to their perfect state,
He walked as if he had never been lame.

Now, that man could enter the temple of the Lord,
He jumped and praised God, his liberator.
All the people saw him and got amazed,
They recognized him as the same who was lame.

The life of that man was never the same,
He lived a supernatural cure through Jesus' name.
The Lord gave him back his happiness and dignity,
The Almighty God gave his liberty.

Heavy Burdens

We go through life carrying heavy burdens,
There are many desires, preoccupations, and fears.
All this makes our souls terribly burdened.

We feel that each day is getting worse the situation,
We feel the burden is becoming unsupportable.
Our hearts melt and fall into desperation.

This giant weight overshadows any and all happiness,
The mind no longer believes something good will happen.
The mind inhabits a deep pit, living in the darkness.

There is a point that is impossible to live in this way,
We fall to the ground, and the weep floods our being.
Everything is so terrible that we even desire to pass away.

In dense darkness, we hear someone calling,
Someone is saying our name.
We look around to see who is speaking.

It is calling That One who can rescue us,
The marvelous, the mighty, the faithful, the great master.
Jesus Christ calls on us, and from the pit, He will take us.

The Lord Jesus Christ illuminates and dissipates darkness,
He holds our hands and raises us.
Through a straight and enlightened way, He will drive us.

That mortal burden, Jesus Christ removes,
He throws away all bad things.
And He gives us His load which is very smooth.

Besides the relief, He always will be by our side,
He will never leave that we follow without aid.
He will never let us fall discouraged another time.

Whenever the load seems heavy again,
Jesus will provide us with His infinite strength.
We will overcome any and all circumstances.

Parked

Many times, we do not see anything happening.
We feel that our world has stopped its motion,
On all sides, everything is in the same position.
Everything seems static; nothing is moving.

The lack of movement produces some agitation.
We cry out desperately for the help of the Lord,
We incessantly seek His grace and favor.
We desire His immediate action in our situation.

We get afflicted when our miracle does not happen.
We continue asking God fervently,
Our mind is dominated by the dreamed blessing.
Our heart dreams about what will be given.

Time passes, and our lives still have not changed.
All the things keep in the same state,
We are sure that there is no blessing in our way.
We feel the Lord has forgotten us; we were abandoned.

Disappointment reaches such a point that we stop praying.
We imagine that will not arrive in our lives,
We believe we will never see that awesome time.
We believe that our dream will never take place.

Suddenly, when we are not even waiting.
Our world begins to move quickly,
Something marvelous happens almost instantaneously.
Our entire situation is transforming.

We understand that God started His work.
New things are created where there was nothing,
An enormous job of God is running.
The Lord fulfilled the desire of our hearts.

We are flooded with a feeling of thankfulness.
We understand that we were unfaithful and impatient,
We act like unbelievers; people without faith.
We notice our mistakes and beg for forgiveness.

We are forgiven thanks to the mercies of the Lord.
We change our thought and posture,
Before God, we will have a new conduct.
We start a new phase with more faith and love.

Requesting Correctly

Everybody has some innermost wish,
Everyone requests God some blessing.
The requests are something very usual,
People need and want to see the supernatural.

Some cry out to the Lord for their healing,
Others cry out to get other types of help from Him.
Believers know that God is Almighty,
For His people, He can do everything.

And among all kinds of requests,
There is one that God does not like to hear it.
God does not like to hear selfish pleas,
Those to receive many useless life's banalities.

Instead of someone requesting a more expensive car,
They should request to become a Lord's clay jar.
Instead of requesting a gigantic mansion,
They should request for those who die of starvation.

People get close to God with meaningless supplications,
Things that have nothing to do with Christ's Kingdom.
Many times, people beg for what will please only them,
Not taking into account the benefits besides them.

Christians must request what is admirable,
Their requests must be pure and respectable.
Requests that can glorify the name of the Lord,
Requests that reflect His glory and splendor.

Each one must ask to be a sharp tool,
To spread on Earth peace, love, and all that is good.
Everyone shall long for Gospel growing,
Then, God will open the sky with a rain of blessings.

Remembering What Happened

All things are very hard,
Will I be capable of overcoming them?
Will I see happy days again?
Will happiness be reached by my hand?

These questions always come to mind,
We think about them when we are desperate.
It seems to be no hope or providence,
We lost our faith and self–confidence.

Right now, something must happen.
We must remember what has already happened to us.
We must bring to mind blessings received,
Bringing to heart all the battles we have triumphed.

In life, everyone has victories to celebrate.
Everybody has many moments of happiness.
Moments which we enjoyed with intensity,
Times when we have lived with felicity.

These were the gifts received by the Lord.
God is always caring about our way.
The Lord was ahead in all the battles,
He frequently shows that never fails.

Even though the current situation is challenging,

We can prostrate and live on weep.

We must keep faith the provision is coming,

Hanging on the assurance of our blessing.

God has already blessed us many times,

It will not be now when He will fail.

Believe boldly in the reply of the Lord,

At the right time, He will give His magnificent favor.

Keep Believing

There is so much time since I heard your promise,
It has been an endless wait since I heard your voice.
I am waiting for everything you have said,
I am anxious to see the transformation in my way.

O Lord! I need your mighty help immediately!
All promised blessings, I want to see.
I feel that all things in my life are frozen,
I feel there is no solution for any of them.

Help me to overcome all the troubles,
Going ahead in my situation is a real struggle.
There are moments when I want to give everything up,
The problems are tough and try to tear me up.

Every day, I always do my best,
But there is no end to this test.
Lord, remember this poor and needed soul,
Act in my life and make this servant grow.

I pray and sing trying to lift my faith,
Always believing that God will make a new way.
I am sure that there is no use to complain,
Surely, complaints will not relieve my pain.

It does not matter what comes against me,

I know the Lord Almighty is for me.

Even if raising thousands of enemies,

With the Lord's help, I will be able to win.

Even all the people saying I will not be blessed,

I will not hear them; God has the final answer.

He is the only one who can decide my destiny,

And I know a river of blessing will come from Him.

As I believed, God made something great,

Where there was nothing; He created.

The Lord fulfilled all His promised words,

He showed me that He is a God of favor.

Gifting

We got satisfied when we receive something,
We love when we are gifted,
We love when our desires are fulfilled.

Gaining something makes us feel important,
We feel that we are dear and beloved,
By other people, we are being remembered.

The gifts are a demonstration of love,
They show that we are worthy of attention,
They say that we deserve consideration.

As we receive love from others,
We must also demonstrate our love and honor,
We must give others our grace and favor.

We must seed that we already have received,
We do not need to start with something material,
We can begin visiting sick people at a hospital.

We can give a piece of attention to someone,
Bringing a little joy to a lonely person,
Showing that they can count on someone.

We can donate our time to hear,
Being attentive to what the other wants to say,
The inner healing, this can generate.

We can also dedicate ourselves to others,
Helping them with their necessities,
Small actions produce huge felicity.

Another manner of helping is through prayer,
Presenting to God the requirements of someone,
This sacrifice is more valuable than a precious stone.

The recognition can be shown with money,
Donating and helping those are more needed,
They will feel immensely blessed.

These were only some examples of seeds,
There are many fields where they can be planted,
They wait for someone for sowing them.

Do your best to improve the world,
God always does His best for everyone,
Let us try to imitate Him with our best effort.

Thinking

God created us with many capabilities,
The Lord gave us many abilities.
Among all our gifts, we have the thinking,
An awesome ability that can do amazing things.

The Creator gave us extraordinary intelligence,
He projected the brain like a perfect masterpiece.
A set of connections very mighty,
A strong organ able to rule over the body.

Besides the body, the brain must reason,
He must analyze what is the right action.
Amid infinity and uncountable options,
We must use wisdom in our decisions.

God can help us with what we must select,
But each one is responsible to elect.
The Lord will not indicate each step of our way,
He already gave us the wisdom to make our best journey.

We must trust in God after each decision,
Trusting that He will be with us in this direction.
The Master will help us to overcome all the difficulties,
He holds our hands throughout all adversities.

Life's Luggage

Throughout life, we receive much luggage,
There are many suitcases and packages to carry,
There are many loads that we always go bearing.

Many of these loads are useful,
The suitcases carry learned experiences,
They carry teachings for all life's moments.

However, we have some useless loads,
Some of them are full of suffering,
When we touch them, we feel awful feelings.

These loads prevent us from going in peace,
They always pull us back to past times,
They never let us achieve the future we desire.

Some of these loads are ingrained in the heart,
They are connected to the deepest of our beings,
We feel that it is impossible to get free from this thing.

We need help from that one who gives freedom,
That one who can break all chains and prisons,
We need the Lord to free our minds and emotions.

He will cut all strings that tie us to the past,
God will deliver us of that suffocate us,
We will walk free; nothing will be arresting us.

All negative and unproductive loads will be removed,
We will carry only things to help in our way,
We will achieve a new and marvelous place.

We will be where the Lord had planned,
A place where His perfect willing reigns,
Where live peace and happiness.

Preoccupations

Preoccupation is something natural for human beings,
Everyone preoccupies with what will happen.
Everyone desires to know how the future will be,
Everyone wants to be ready for tomorrow.

This search for preparation can generate anxiety,
The mind is filled with an infinity of imagination.
One creates inside themselves all types of scenarios,
Each person imagines everything that can take place.

These imaginations turn into a kind of fear,
They root in the heart and produce anguish.
The person is concerned all the time; there is no rest.
They get restless and without knowing what to do.

And for most of the time, the preoccupation is useless,
Because these are things that nobody can predict.
One experiences anticipated and meaningless suffering,
The suffering is based only on expectancy.

It is needed help to be freed from anxiety,
The person must look high and ask for help.
They must remember that one who controls all,
They must remember there is an Almighty God.

This God is able to relieve this heavy anguish,
He will take off preoccupation, fear, and anxiety.
The person will live in peace with himself again,
They will smile again and have faith in a better future.

The Lord brings an inexplicable and endurance peace,
Even if destiny shows itself totally uncertain.
God calms the heart giving it confidence,
Giving it great hope amid the chaos.

Whenever the person thinks to get desperate,
They will remember there is no reason for this.
The person will deliver their anxieties to the Lord,
And they will rest waiting for His marvelous action.

Spoken Words

People like to talk about me,
They say bad words against me.

They say words to despise me,
They say things to devalue me.

All people do this freely,
Exposing their minds are malign.

The tongues are very malicious,
They are like poisonous cobras.

Their only mission is destroying me,
They span venom to wound me.

I will protect myself from all this,
There will be a shield in my ears.

The poisoned word, I will not listen,
Good words; I will speak a ton of them.

My mouth is a source of blessing,
They will say what is the heart's pleasing.

My words will always be beautiful,
With life, they will always be full.

I will declare words of encouragement and victory,
I will state how my story will be.

I will speak of the wonders of the Lord,
I will worship His love and favor.

I will sing of the plans of my God,
I will sing I am a son of the Sovereign Lord.

I will give thanks because He has saved me,
I will give thanks for the life He gave me.

Good will be spread from my lips,
Undoing all the evil words and deeds.

The blessing will win curse and condemnation,
And my good words will be my protection.

From Darkness to Light

On that darkest night,
Everything was icy.
All was darkness and shadow,
No light could be seen.

My world was full of disillusionment,
I did not have any love or peace.
I lived in chaos and sadness,
I was submerged in pain and agony.

I did not want to stay alive,
I could not continue living like that.
I wanted to die immediately,
I desired my death.

In the darkness, light shone,
I was called gently.
Someone cared about my life,
Someone wanted to be with me.

A mighty hand was extended,
I grabbed it with much determination.
I feel that was a new chance,
I could change my situation.

The hand of God lifted me,
He took me off from that place.
The Lord showed me hope,
He lifted me with His grace.

I left that terrible world,
My life has been renewed.
Now, I live happily and with peace,
My story has been transformed.

I am proof of the power of God,
He can turn around any life.
I introduce Him to other people,
So that, they also can rise.

The Day

Each morning, my mind is renewed,

I declare that my day will be blessed.

I ask for God that His grace be poured,

I give thanks for everything He has granted.

I fill my mind with positive thoughts,

I consider this day another gift from the Lord.

I move away from me all negative thoughts,

I am already thankful for the blessings prepared by God.

These attitudes direct my whole day,

They allow me to have another vision.

I recognize God caring about my way,

I thank Him for His endless love and protection.

Whenever I can, I talk to the Lord,

I remember all His mercies.

I give thanks for His awesome favor,

I give thanks to have another day of victory.

At the end of the day, I thank the Lord again,

I give thanks for all the received blessings.

I give thanks for His permanent caring,

I ask for more blessings for the day that is coming.

Help to Continue

When all say you should stop dreaming,
When all indicate that you should stop trying,
When all is against you and wants to destroy you,
When it is hard and the will to give up dominates you.

Remember: there are reasons to continue,
There is hope and strength to help you.
You were not abandoned; you do not go alone,
By your side is the Lord, the Mighty One.

You and the great God are mighty and unbeatable,
Fighting alongside the Lord makes you invincible.
Nothing will be able to stop your determination,
Nobody will have forces to interrupt your mission.

Go ahead and fight bravely until you win,
God's infinite power is upon you.
The Lord blesses you and gives you victory,
He is writing a wonderful story.

What God Says

The world says, "You can't do it; you don't deserve it."
And God says, "You can do everything; you deserve it!"

The world says, "You don't matter, give up."
And God says, "You are precious, go ahead!"

The world says, "Nobody will love you."
And God says, "I will always love you."

The world says, "You'll never overcome it."
And God says, "Surely, you will overcome it!"

The world says, "You'll never be healed."
And God says, "You will be healed and restored!"

The world says, "You'll never break this addiction."
And God says, "You will break it and have a new life!"

The world says, "Your past is a shadow upon your life."
And God says, "I will write a new story for you!"

The world says, "This business will never prosper."
And God says, "I will prosper everything you do!"

The world says, "You'll never get this promotion."
And God says, "I will put you in a higher position!"

The world says, "You'll always keep failing."
And God says, "I will lead you to victory!"

The world says, "You've sinned and are condemned."
And God says, "I will erase all your sins!"

The world says, "Nobody in your family could do it."
And God says, "You will do great works!"

The world says, "Don't believe in empty promises."
And God says, "I will fulfill all I have promised you!"

Do not hear what the world says,
Hear only what God says.

My Failure

I did everything right and didn't get the win,
I worked hard all my days.
Now, all seems in vain and meaningless,
I didn't notice any improvement in anything.

I try to understand what I did wrong,
I seek explanations, reasons, and justifications.
I analyze each detail to understand,
For this failure, I need to know its reason.

My search led me nowhere,
I still don't understand what happened.
I still don't accept the defeat I lived,
To keep going, I need answers.

I opened my heart before the Lord,
I poured out all my anguish and sadness.
I ask Him for an answer to my doubt,
Something totally unexpected, He showed me.

God made me see something I'd never imagined,
He showed me that my failure was not in vain.
God's wisdom shone on me,
I understood the purpose of my life.

Failure taught me to be strong and brave,
Misfortune gave me the wisdom to carry on.
Defeat showed me another path to follow,
This situation taught me to move on.

I lift my head to face the future,
Don't matter what'll come; I know that God is with me.
Even if I fail again, I won't be discouraged,
With God, I can beat the whole world; we're the majority.

Two Ways

There are two pieces of advice for our lives,
One of them comes from the Lord, the Mighty One,
And the other comes from the Devil, the Evil One.

The words of the Lord are pleasant and good,
The words of the Evil One are bad and harmful.
He tries to deceive you in all you think or try to do.

He perverts the holy paths the Lord has made,
He wants to lead people to disgrace.
But in everything, he shows the best face.

He will not exhibit something unattractive,
He will make your eyes shine for you to believe.
You will think: "For sure, I need this."

The Devil continues enticing and seducing you,
More and more, he is capturing you.
You cannot notice what you are turning into.

You are away from the Lord; you are poor and blind,
You even cannot see; you are far from the light.
For you, it does not matter the ways of your life.

However, the Mighty One will never give up,
His unfailing and eternal love, He will show up.
From the darkest and deepest well, He will lift you up.

God will break all yokes, strings, and chains,
You will see the enlightened path again.
Your life will be under God's command.

After all, you will regret all you did,
You will ask God's pardon for all this.
In His immense mercy, He will erase your sins.

You will start a new life in the right way,
You will never want to get astray.
You tasted how terrible it is to move away.

Substituting Thoughts

All of us carry many thoughts,
We carry what we learned through life.

Many thoughts are good for us,
However, others are disturbing us.

We must substitute unfavorable thoughts,
We must replace them with victorious thoughts.

Instead of saying, "I can't do this."
You must say, "Yes, I can do it."

Instead of saying, "I always lived in this way."
You must say, "I'll switch to a better way."

Instead of saying, "I'll face a long and hard day."
You must say, "Thank you, Lord, I'm alive another day."

Instead of saying, "What a bad and terrible day!"
You must say, "Thank you, Lord; I overcame this day."

Instead of saying, "I give up! All is an endless mess!"
You must say, "I'll fix everything; I'll do my best."

Instead of saying, "All always ends in nothing."
You must say, "All I do will have a happy ending."

Instead of saying, "This sickness is part of me."
You must say, "This sickness doesn't belong to me."

Instead of saying, "I'll never find the right person."
You must say, "I'll find the perfect person."

Instead of saying, "This crisis will affect me and everyone."
You must say, "I'm safe under God's protection."

Instead of saying, "My business isn't working."
You must say, "I already see my business growing."

If you change your thoughts, all will be different,
You will change your attitude because of your statement.

You will believe in yourself and God,
You will work and receive the blessing of the Lord.

The Flame Almost Extinguished

I started my Christian run very encouraged,
For all kinds of work, I was ready.
Nobody could disturb or discourage me.
I was wherever there was a need.

I felt a strong desire to help in all things,
In all God's works, I wanted to be supporting.
To do this gave me purpose and satisfaction,
I did it all with a colossal disposition.

I went to church on all occasions,
I prayed to God in all the situations.
I praised the Lord during my whole time,
I gave thanks for His blessings upon my life.

I continued my journey, and my spirit got discouraged,
I no longer worked with the same love.
Everything turned into an obligation,
I no longer acted with zeal or passion.

The flame in my heart extinguished,
I did not even talk to the Lord.
My heart did not wish His presence,
I was Christian only in appearance.

I did not know precisely what had happened,
However, I knew that something had been altered.
I was not satisfied with my living way,
And what if I did not do anything, I would pass away.

I claimed to the Lord desperately,
An enlightened mind, I begged Him.
God kindly tranquilized me,
And the right way, He pointed at me.

I must pray and remember the blessings,
I must remember His commandments and teachings.
I must follow His word of life in all my days,
Acknowledging the excellence in His ways.

I shall remember the promises of the Lord,
I must remember His tremendous love and favor.
So, I will always be encouraged and full of energy,
The flame of my life is lit by the Holy Spirit.

A flame that will shine brightly,
A light that will live eternally.
With God, my bright will never be extinguished,
The Lord's light will always blaze on me.

Thanks in Advance

Lord God, I give thanks for what will come,
I thank the Lord for what will go on.
I thank the Lord for everything I cannot see,
I am thankful for all that God is preparing for me.

I give God thanks no matter the situation,
I give Him thanks for His tremendous operation.
I give thanks because God acts constantly,
I always thank Him for my future blessings.

I thank Him because I know that God is at work now,
I am thankful because He is setting my perfect hour.
I give thanks because I wholeheartedly trust in Him,
I give thanks because He is the owner of my destiny.

I am grateful because I know who the Lord is,
I am thankful for His kindness that will come as a sea.
I thank Him even before I have received,
I am grateful because I know I have already been blessed.

Thank you, Lord, for keeping my heart serene,
I thank God because I know what silence means.
I give thanks to God for all things He will deliver me,
I thank every new thing He is bringing upon me.

From Preoccupation to Peace

I wake up, and it starts the preoccupation
I have no peace but agitation
I get agitated thinking: what will come?
I get nervous imagining: what will go on?
My nerves are troubled
All my being is very exalted.

I live like that all the days
There is no peace in my ways
I'm always fatigued
I'm completely exhausted
I have no strength for anything
My flame is decreasing.

I need help to free me
Someone who can relieve me
I need a merciful hand
Someone to bring me to the promised land
I need to get out of this prison
Someone who gives me liberation.

There is only one who can do this
Someone able to understand me
The Lord God can save me
He'll free me from the anguish
I'll be able to walk carefree
He'll relieve me from what was heavy.

I'll deliver to the Lord my preoccupation
He will lead me to a solution
That seemed totally impossible
With God converts into possible
I'll continue trusting in His great help,
I know that I'm not alone in my battle.

The mighty hand of God will cover me
From the evils, He'll protect me
To infinite peace, He'll lead me
A new life will begin
Leaving all stress and preoccupation
Living confidently in the God of my salvation.

Not Yet

Hearing "not yet" is not the same as not.
It does not mean that we will not achieve,
It does not mean that we will not succeed,
It does not mean we will not improve,
It does not mean we will not make a move.

Hearing "not yet" can be discouraging,
It can be extremely disheartening,
It may be that we feel depressed,
We may be downcast.
Everything seems to be meaningless,
It seems that God will not grant our request.

Hearing "not yet" generates sadness.
We feel that all is stopped,
We feel our miracle will not be performed.
We feel great frustration,
We feel a huge dissatisfaction.

Hearing "not yet" has some meaning.
It means that the moment is not yet,
It means it is not our time yet.
It means that we still cannot receive,
It means we must learn something before we achieve.

Hearing God say "not yet" is something positive.
He shows that we need preparation,
It shows He wants to bless our situation,
It shows the Lord wants to help us,
The Lord is willing to perfect us.

When we are ready, the answer will be "yes".
We will enjoy the gigantic blessing of the Lord,
We will receive that so dreamed favor.
All will be in its perfect place,
And we will be able to administrate.

"The Saints"

Many Christians are living isolated
They are in their worlds, living separated
From all the sins, they are "protected".

They are imprisoned inside a building
Their only desire is to go to the meeting
They want to hear sweet and happy preaching.

They forgot about the world outside
They forgot where the sinner resides
They do not preach the Lord to save lives.

On their salvation, many are sitting
They think they have the perfect anointing
With other lives, they have no caring.

Whenever this happens, God creates a solution
The Lord will touch a heart to go into action
He will show them His splendorous salvation.

This life will find the Lord
And they will know His love and favor
Then, they will act like a pastor.

The person will return to where they were
They will show other God's word power
In this way, people will be saved.

While other people are caged
The new Christian goes out and works
Too many lives are changed.

The sinners are forgiven and freed
And "the saints" are condemned
Religion has left them enslaved.

Need for Cleaning

Like a house, life must be cleaned
An everyday deep cleaning must happen
We must rid ourselves of what can dirt us
Then, we can reach holiness.

Sometimes, the dirt is not enormous,
It is not something flashy or monstrous
It can be bits that are dirtying us
A small thing that is disturbing us.

This small thing can be swearing words
Some always say these kinds of bad words
It can be that lustful glance
Producing desires that are so intense.

There are some dirtied by bad behavior
They always show a bad temper.
They are too severe in their response and actions
They think they are perfect in all situations.

Others are dirty with lies
Big or small, they are part of their lives
Their words are loaded with falsehood
They distort what should be truthful.

These and other little things are harmful
They take us away from God, our Father.
They may seem minimal and harmless things
However, they are deteriorating our way of living.

All that is bad must be discarded
What was dirty must be cleaned
If there is any difficulty to do it
One must cry out to the Lord to help with it.

God will help during the organization
He will give a new heart to the person
They will be free from what was dirty
Their lives will be completely renewed.

The new life will be closer to the Lord
Closer to His abundant blessings, love, and favor
The person will experience great happiness
They will live with God in holiness.

No Excuses

"I can't! I don't get it!
Everything is against me!
All the people hate me.
Nobody wants to help me."

These words show immaturity
And are loaded with self–pity.
The person set that situation
And they believe in their imagination.

These thoughts limit their actions
These beliefs affect their decisions.
The person does not see any escape
They accepted living in a suffering way.

This unhappy situation must change immediately
The person must alter their mind and vocabulary.
They need to seek to become successful,
They must fight for all their dreams to come true.

It is the time to take responsibility
It is the only way to change reality.
There is no point in standing still and complaining
There is no success for those who live down in spirit.

The person must stop with any excuse
They must get up and bravely fight.
This is the only way to development
It is the only way to get new achievements.

Some help will be necessary during the fight
Someone will be needed to protect their life.
There is only one able to face everything
There is only one able to keep them advancing.

Only the Lord God can help them
Only the Lord can strengthen them.
With God's help, everything will be overpowered
A victorious character will be forged.

Never again will depressive words be said
That will be dead; it will seem like another life instead.
There will be trust and protection from the Lord
Even if there are struggles, there will be His favor.

My Garden

I have a precious garden; I must take care of it,
A special place where I must work on it.
My heart is an exceptional soil
There can be sown the good and evil.

The garden flourishes when good is sown
Love and hope sprout and grow.
Kindness spreads out in all directions
There are excellent fruits in trees of emotions.

I look at the garden and see its sublime perfection
I feel peace of mind and joy in my heart.
It is being poured out, a rain of blessings
God's water makes new things.

However, some intruders may arrive
In the darkness and shadows, they try to hide.
They are the enemies of the garden of my life
Destruction of my happiness is their only desire.

They trample and cut the plants, and spread vileness
Trying exhaustively to kill happiness.
They want all kindness to be uprooted
They want to see the dry drought, lifeless, deserted.

There arrived disguised many of these enemies.
They said they would help me.
They promised they would always be with me
They promised they were friends of me

They were sent by the destroyer, the evil one
He is the great enemy of the Lord, the Mighty One.
He cannot see good on the earth
He soon sends his servants to disturb.

Greater than the enemy of the garden is its Creator
Greater than evil is the goodness of the Lord.
Even if the enemy sends his whole army
They are not more than insects before the Almighty.

The Lord will drive away all evil from my garden
Even if plagues come, I will destroy them.
God will take care of my heart every day
Showing His infinite kindness over my life and way.

God's Promises

God promised Noah to preserve him and his family,
He trusted and did everything just as God commanded.
After the floodwaters, the promise was fulfilled.

God promised a son to Abraham and Sara in old age,
They trusted in the Lord to change their way.
The promise was fulfilled in Isaac; they had a baby.

God promised Isaac blessings to his descendants,
He trusted in the Lord, and they possessed Canaan.
The promise was fulfilled; God gave them a new land.

God promised Jacob that He will be with him,
He trusted in the Lord during his entire journey.
The promise was fulfilled; he defeated his enemies.

God promised Joseph that he would rule over everyone,
He trusted in the Lord that his breakthrough would come.
The promise was fulfilled; In Egypt, he was the second one.

God promised Moses he would free Israel from slavery land,
He trusted in the Lord and saw His mighty hand.
The promise was fulfilled; he led people to Canaan.

God promised Gideon he would free the Israelites,
He trusted in the Lord and went to the fight.
The promise was fulfilled; he defeated the Midianites.

God promised David an everlasting offspring and kingdom,
He trusted in the Lord, and his wife bore him Salomon.
The promise was fulfilled through the life of his son.

God promised Elijah that it would rain again,
He trusted the Lord would send his blessing to the land.
The promise was fulfilled; God opened the heavens.

God promised Naaman he would be cleansed of leprosy,
He trusted in the Lord's prophet even being angry.
The promise was fulfilled; the Lord healed him.

God has too many promises in the Bible,
And He has been fulfilling all of them since the principle.
God is always acting in the lives of His people.

We are God's people, and He is acting on us,
We only need to believe in what He promised us.
All His promises and blessings will come upon us.

Definitive Sacrifice

We are already free; nobody can condemn us,
We already have been chosen and separated by God,
Jesus shed His blood to save us.

He suffered a terrible punishment instead of us,
He did everything to show His infinite love.
He did His best to forgive us.

Christ's sacrifice is something unmatched,
No other thing has the same value,
God's love for His people is unequaled.

What Jesus Christ did was a definitive action,
A unique and sufficient sacrifice,
An expiatory act that does not need repetition.

His precious blood covers all the sins,
As a river of pure waters that cleanse each one.
It does not matter if they are past or future sins.

All that we did or will do is forgiven,
God gifted us like that because He knows us,
He knows that we are not immune to sin.

We may fail even with our best efforts,

There is always the possibility of falling into temptation,

All mankind is subject to sin and errors.

What if that takes place, we have a Savior,

We have the blood of Christ to forgive us,

Then, we will live in peace with the Lord.

The Summons

God is calling all the people
He is summoning everybody who can hear.
He desires everyone to get close
He expects everyone to know Him.

God is kind and compassionate
He is always seeking His sons.
It does not matter where they are
God loves them and cries out his names.

Even in the darkest shadows
Or in the deepest darkness.
The Lord God will extend His hand
He will take out his sons to light.

Even the son who is living in sin
The Lord will not reject him.
God will show the right way
And He will wait for him with open arms.

God only desires repentance
He desires a change in the mind and heart.
The Lord does not require anything but this
By doing it, the person will become his son.

The Lord wants to get close to His family
He desires everyone to recognize His parenthood.
All will be different being close to Him
Life will not be the same as before.

The person will live with happiness and love
Living days that they had never dreamed of.
All is possible for those who choose to change
All is possible for those who live with God.

The Road

Life is a large road
An extensive way to be traveled
A journey with many highs and lows
An adventure towards our destiny.

Sometimes, this way is calm
Dominated by an incredible peacefulness
All happens wonderfully
We follow through the trail of happiness.

Other times, the way is troubled
There are difficulties to keep up
We face many obstacles
There are moments we consider to give up.

Sometimes, we feel all is stopped
We parked in the middle of the highway
We seek for a direction, an indication
We cannot see a future for our way.

Life's road demands wisdom,
It requires a strong and patient heart
We must be attentive to details,
Never give up and always move forward.

We must trust the constructor of the road
We must lean on that one that created everything
Our sure must be in the Lord God
The owner of our life, the world's road, and its things.

He is the only one who has a complete map
The only one who knows all directions
He knows precisely where we must go
He gets us calm amid the chaos of tribulations.

Let us deliver the conduction to the Lord
He will lead us in His best street
Caring for each one of the steps
Until we arrive at the perfect destiny.

Seeking Acknowledgment

We want to be recognized,
We desire to be applauded,
We long to be noticed,
We want to be valued.

We fight for something to happen,
We battle to get people's acknowledgment.
We dream about that amazing occasion,
On which we will have a great reputation.

These wishes are natural,
Everybody wants to feel special,
To feel there is a purpose in what is done,
To feel that we are the best ones.

However, it seems we are invisible,
It seems we are contemptible.
Nobody gives us a piece of attention,
Nobody shows any consideration.

All that is done seems vainly,
This sensation is heartbreaking.
We did our best in everything,
And we only receive apathy.

The pain blinds our comprehension,
We forget who is seeing our actions.
We forget for whom we are working,
It is not for a simple human being.

We are working to the Lord,
He sees us with immeasurable value.
Even if nobody gives us attention,
God applauds our dedication.

God is a witness to all we did,
He comprehends our feelings.
The Father gives us strength to continue,
And many more things, we will execute.

We must calm ourselves and rest,
We know who waits our best.
Let us do our best effort to the Lord,
He will pour out upon us His abundant favor.

Rest and Sin

"Not today, but tomorrow I'll do everything,
A little rest, then, I'll be ready for this.
Don't hurry up, you don't need to get concerned,
Tomorrow or later, everything will be executed."

There is a serious sin in these words,
They are creating gaps to escape from work.
Those sayings exude procrastination,
They poison the mind with a sweet illusion.

The body is assaulted by laziness,
Working in a permanent state of slowness.
The mind gets happy about this condition,
They think this is a favorable situation.

The procrastinator's life is being thrown away,
They are wasting each one of their days.
Negating the great gifts they received,
Rejecting everything that God has conceded.

God gave them a spectacular mind,
Infinite imaginations they can find.
The Lord gave them a majestic body,
The perfect complement for their mind.

The procrastinator dishonors their Creator,
They despise the Lord's plan and effort.
This person lives without reverence,
Acting complete and utter negligence.

The need for change is urgent and undeniable,
The person needs to be responsible.
Fleeing from laziness and procrastination,
Hugging the effort and dedication.

God will forgive and reward them,
The sources of blessings will be open.
The person will live what they never imagined,
All will take place because they worked.

Enormous fruits will be generated,
Marvelous miracles will be collected.
There will be no room for poverty,
They will live in abundance and prosperity.

Acrostics

Person

Able to introduce

Salvation

To

Others and help to

Rescue them

Announcing with a

Daring attitude

Our miracles

Received being

Enthusiastically

Prostrating to hear God's voice

Revealing Him our wishes and fears

Adoring the Lord with gratitude for all

Your blessings and promises received

About the Author

Rafael Henrique dos Santos Lima

Associate Degree in Administration and M.B.A. in Strategic Project Management by Centro Universitário UNA. Christian by the grace of God. Passionate about writing (English, Portuguese, Spanish), poet and novelist.

Contacts

rafael50001@hotmail.com

rafaelhsts@gmail.com

Instagram: @rafael.lima.poeta

Blog: escritorrafaellima.blogspot.com

Acknowledgements

The following sites contain a lot of useful information for the translation.

Bing

Google Docs

Google Translator

Grammarly

Language Tool

Oxford Dictionary

Rhyme Zone

I thank the websites Playground AI and Bing AI, they were essential for the generation of the book's cover.

Special Acknowledgement

I thank God. He gave me the intelligence to write the poems.